NOTESPELLER STORIES & GAMES

BOOK ONE

AROUND THE WORLD

KAREN HARRINGTON

ISBN 978-1-4584-1784-8

HAL•LEONARD®

Visit Hal Leonard Online at
www.halleonard.com

Contact Us:
Hal Leonard
7777 West Bluemound Road
Milwaukee, WI 53213
Email: info@halleonard.com

In Europe contact:
Hal Leonard Europe Limited
Distribution Centre, Newmarket Road
Bury St Edmunds, Suffolk, IP33 3YB
Email: info@halleonardeurope.com

In Australia contact:
Hal Leonard Australia Pty. Ltd.
4 Lentara Court
Cheltenham, Victoria, 3192 Australia
Email: info@halleonard.com.au

NOTES FOUND IN THE STORIES AND GAMES

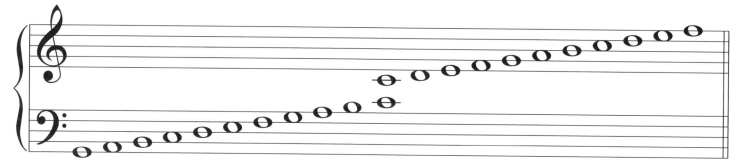

A Message to Students:

As you progress through this notespeller, I hope you will learn not only the notes of the staff but also some interesting facts about our world. I have had a good time writing this book, creating stories for you to complete and puzzles for you to solve. Have a good time and make learning and music important parts of your life.

ACKNOWLEDGEMENTS: Thanks to Jennifer Linn for her ideas, expertise, and encouragement and for editing this book. My thanks also goes to my friend and colleague Philelle McBrayer and my husband, John, for their encouragement and help.

ABOUT THE AUTHOR: Karen Harrington, NCTM, maintains a private studio in Tulsa, Oklahoma, where sha has taught piano for over thirty years. A graduate of the University of Oklahoma, she holds a BME degree with piano emphasis. Before opening her independent studio Karen taught music in the Tulsa Public Schools for eight years. She has also taught piano at the University of Tulsa.

Karen served for two years on the board of directors of the Music Teachers National Association. She is currently President Elect of Oklahoma Music Teachers Association and has served as Northeast District President and Vice President. She is a past president of Tulsa Accredited Music Teachers Association and serves as a clinician and adjudicator for her state and local associations. She is a member of Tulsa Piano Study Club.

Through her company Music Games 'N Things, Karen produced music theory games including **Forward March**, **Time Out** and **Perfect Pitch**. For the Hal Leonard Corporation she is co-author of the **Hal Leonard Student Piano Library Piano Theory** workbooks, author of the **Notespellers for Piano**, **Tic-Tac-Toe Music Games** and **Piano Teacher's Resource Kit**.

CONTENTS

Facts About Greece

Write the names of the notes in the shaded boxes to complete the words.

r   is part o   urop   an   on the

o   th A   an S   a.   The flag of   r

is blue and white.   r   is the birthpla   o   th   Olympic

am   s. I   you   i   to   o to   r

visit th   apital, Athens.

4

BASS STAFF C D E F G
More Facts About Greece

Write the names of the notes in the shaded boxes to complete the words.

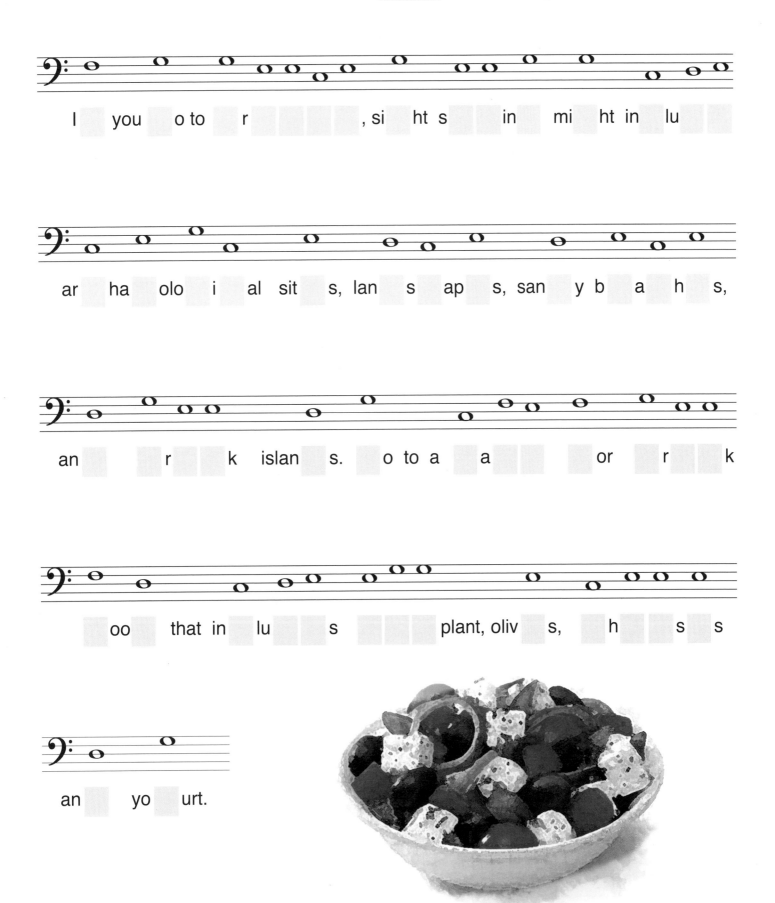

I ___ you ___ o to ___ r ___ ___ ___ ___ , si ___ ht s ___ ___ in ___ mi ___ ht in ___ lu ___ ___

ar ___ ha ___ olo ___ i ___ al sit ___ s, lan ___ s ___ ap ___ s, san ___ y b ___ a ___ h ___ s,

an ___ ___ r ___ k islan ___ s. ___ o to a ___ a ___ ___ or ___ r ___ k

___ oo ___ that in ___ lu ___ s ___ ___ ___ plant, oliv ___ s, ___ h ___ s ___ s

an ___ yo ___ urt.

TREBLE AND BASS STAFFS C D E F G
Sounds Heard 'Round the World

Use the notes from the staffs on page 7 and draw a half note for each letter in a box.
Watch for the treble and bass clef signs.

Str e et c r i e s

g i g g l e s

e c ho e s

Tr a f f i c

Bir d s   c hirpin g

c on c e rts

c hil d r e n   lau g hin g

g e e s e   p e c kin g

f la g s   f lyin g

g ira f f e s f e e d in g

e l e c tri c   g uitars

c ars   ra c in g

DRAWING YOUR OWN NOTES
The International Language

1. Circle each C, D, E, F, G that you find in the text.

2. Use the notes from the staffs below to draw a whole note for each circled letter. Watch the clef signs.

Music is called the international language. From

near and far children are singing, dancing

and playing instruments. Music can make us

wiggle, giggle and laugh. It can make us sad,

glad or describe a mood.

NOTES SURROUNDING MIDDLE C

Some Countries within the Seven Continents

The seven continents are Africa, Asia, Europe, North America, South America, Australia and Antarctica.

To find the names of the countries below, name the notes in the boxes. For more fun write the name of the continent below each country. Find the names of the matching continents at the bottom of this page.

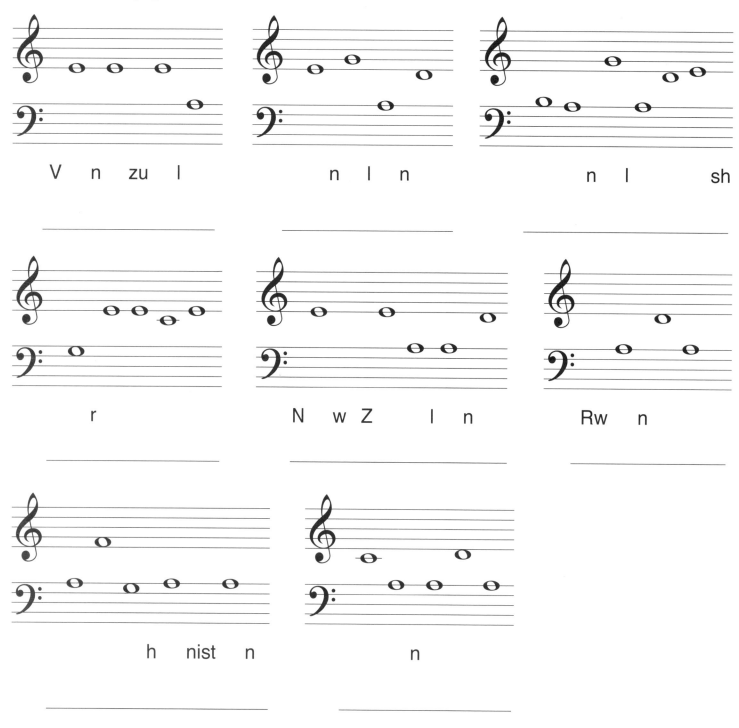

V n zu l

n l n

n l sh

r

N w Z l n

Rw n

h nist n

n

r   ntin   I   l   n   Sw   n

Unit   St   t   s   S   otl   n   or   i

ul   ri   U   n   r   n

Whi   h   ontin   nt is th   ol   st?   nt   r   ti

NOTES SURROUNDING MIDDLE C
The World's Largest Cities

1. Write the names of the notes in the boxes below to complete the names of the world's largest cities.

2. Choose the country of each city from the list and write the name on the line below the city.

Countries: Brazil, Korea, Pakistan, Russia, Turkey, India (use 2 times), and China (use 5 times)

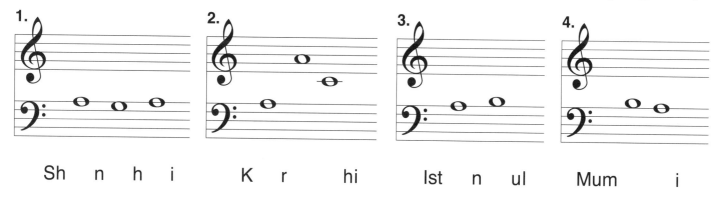

1. Sh □ n □ h □ i

2. K □ r □ hi

3. Ist □ n □ ul

4. Mum □ i

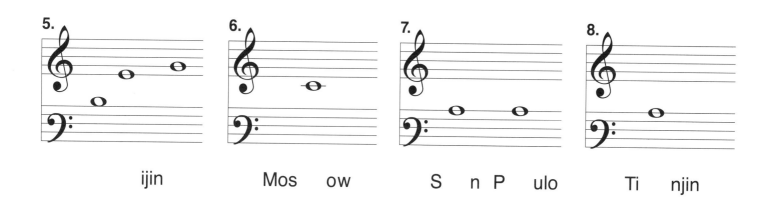

5. □ ijin

6. Mos □ ow

7. S □ n P □ ulo

8. Ti □ njin

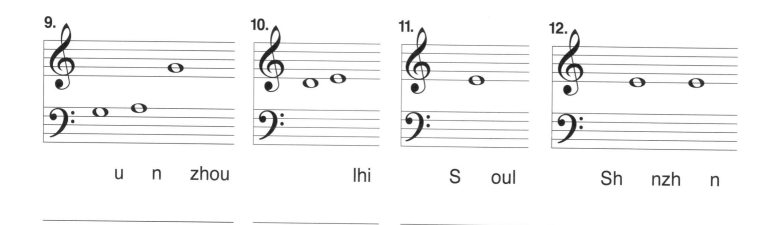

9. □ u □ n □ zhou

10. □ lhi

11. S □ oul

12. Sh □ nzh □ n

NOTES SURROUNDING MIDDLE C
World Landmarks

Write the names of the notes in the shaded boxes to discover the names of some landmarks and their locations.

T☐j☐M☐h☐l☐–☐☐r☐ln☐i

Th☐☐r☐t W☐ll☐–☐hin☐

Sp☐☐☐☐ N☐☐☐l☐ – S☐ttl☐ W☐☐ – US☐

☐u☐☐nh☐im Mus☐ums – ☐il☐o, Sp☐in☐☐n N☐w York

Th☐☐☐i☐☐☐l Tow☐r – P☐ris, ☐r☐n☐

Th☐ P☐rth☐non – ☐th☐ns, ☐r☐☐☐

11

BASS "C" TO TREBLE "C" NOTES
Sightseeing

1. Name each note in the shaded boxes to see what things one might see while traveling.

2. Draw a line from the note to its matching key.

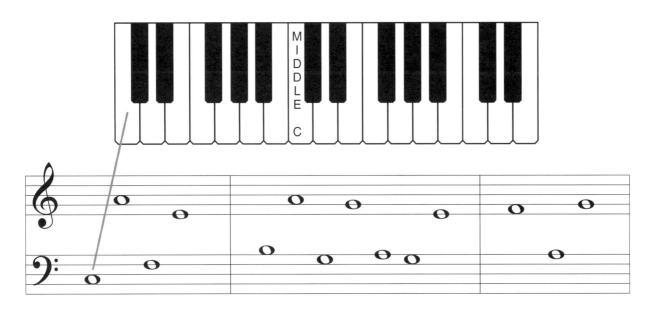

s   l   s

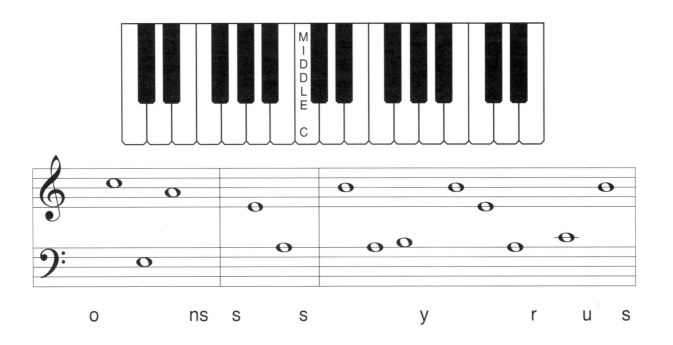

o   ns   s   s   y   r   u   s

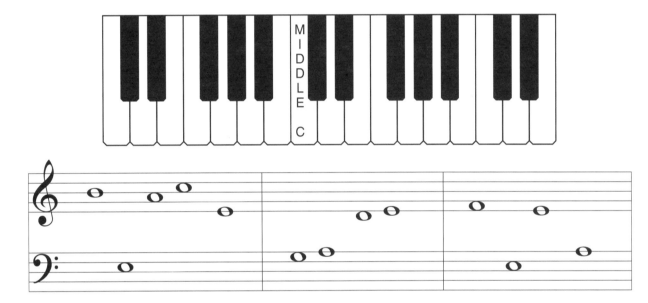

h   s   r   ns   r   w   ys

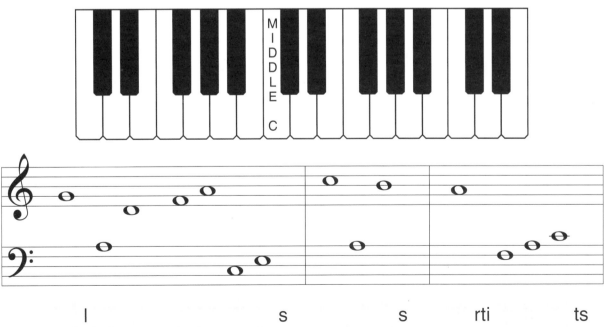

l   s   s   rti   ts

INTERVALS—2NDS
Oceans Around the World

Write the names of the notes in the shaded boxes.

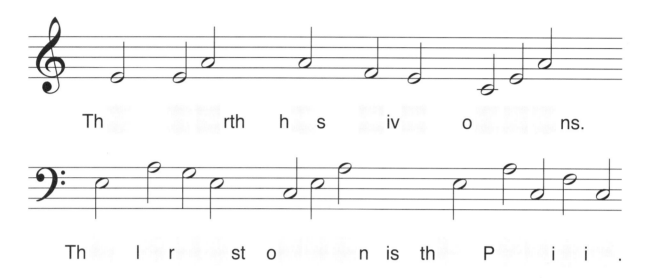

Th ▢ ▢ rth h ▢ s ▢ iv ▢ o ▢ ▢ ns.

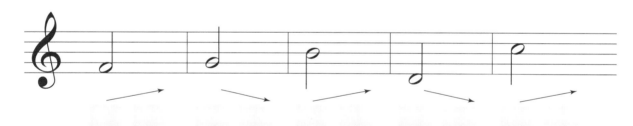

Th ▢ I ▢ r ▢ st o ▢ ▢ n is th ▢ P ▢ i ▢ i ▢ .

Follow the arrows below and draw a note that is a 2nd (step) above or below the given note. Name both notes.

Each staff is named for one of earth's oceans.

The Pacific Ocean

The Indian Ocean

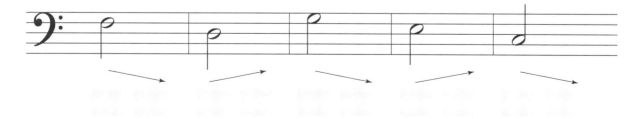

The Arctic Ocean

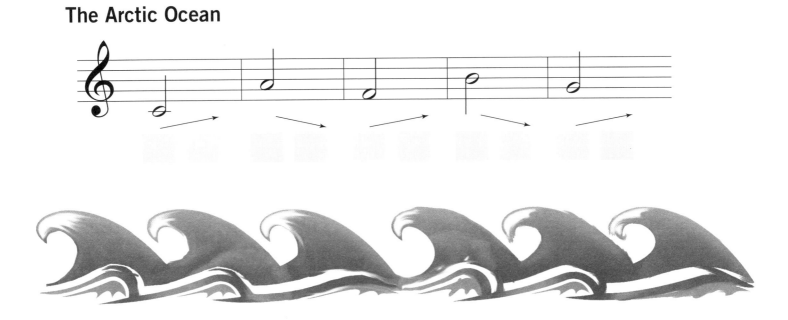

The Atlantic Ocean

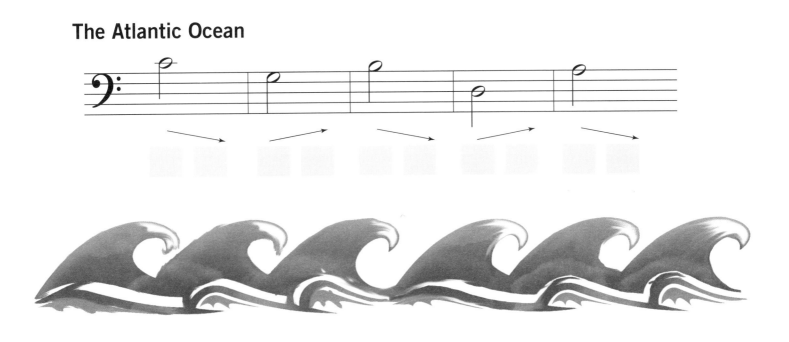

The Southern Ocean

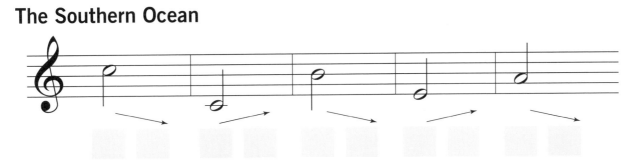

INTERVALS—2NDS
Ocean Jokes

1. Write the names of the notes in the shaded boxes.   2. Circle all of the seconds.

TREBLE AND BASS LINE AND SPACE NOTES

Slogans

Callie and Dan are having a slogan contest for naming the line and space notes for the treble and bass staffs.

1. For each slogan draw the correct clef sign and the line or space notes.

2. Vote for your favorite slogan by circling the one you like the best.

Great Britian Denmark France Asia

All Cars Eat Gas

Australia China Europe Germany

Great Birth - Days For All

Every Good Boy Does Fine

Find A Close Exit

France Austria Canada England

Every Good Band Deserves Fame

Good Boys Do Fine Always

All Cows Eat Grass

Every Gas Boat Drives Fast

F   A   C   E

INTERVALS—3RDS
A River Cruise

1. In the white boxes write the letter name of each note.
2. In the shaded boxes write the letter name of the note that moves up or down by a third.
3. Draw a note for each letter in the shaded box.

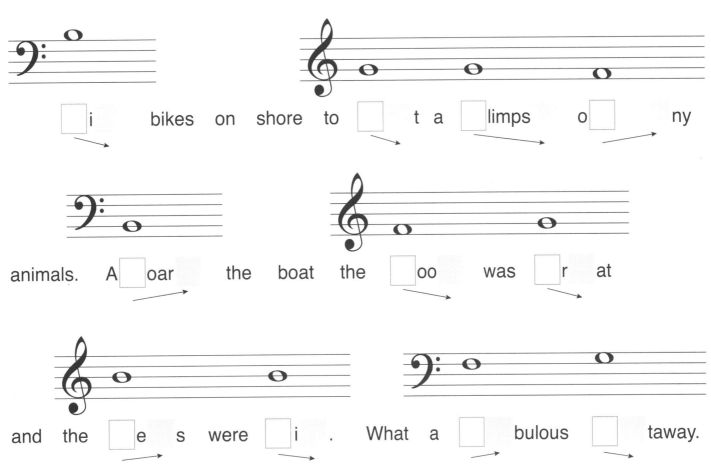

tr [ ] ks   alon [ ] th   bank   we [ ] e [ ] d   to   ride

[ ] i   bikes   on   shore   to [ ] t   a [ ] limps   o [ ] ny

animals.   A [ ] oar   the   boat   the [ ] oo   was [ ] r   at

and   the [ ] e   s   were [ ] i .   What   a [ ] bulous [ ] taway.

TREBLE AND BASS SPACE NOTES
World Amusement Parks and Zoos

Name the notes in the shaded boxes to discover things one might see at a world amusement park or zoo.

TREBLE AND BASS LINE NOTES
A World Art Museum

Name the notes in the shaded boxes to discover things one might see at a world famous art museum.

TREBLE AND BASS LINE AND SPACE NOTES
The Family Takes a Ride

Name the notes to complete the story.

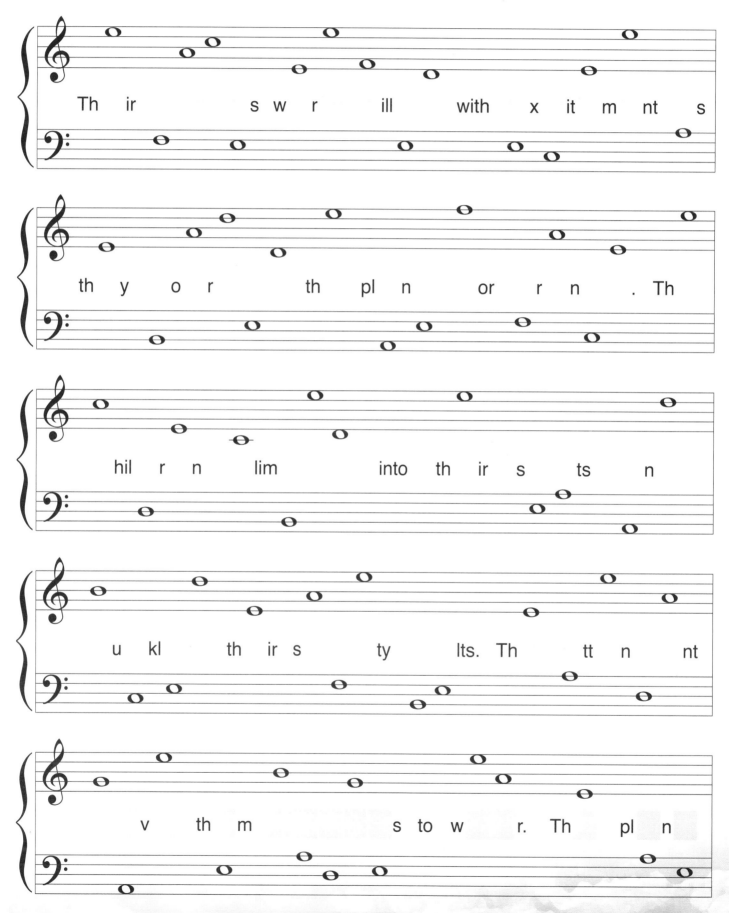

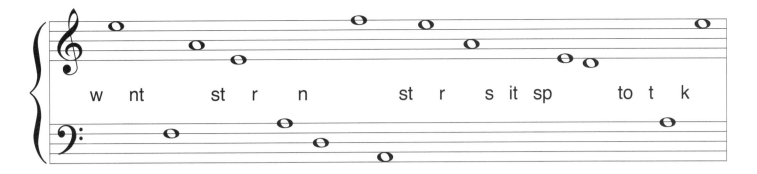

w   nt   st r   n   st r s it sp   to t   k

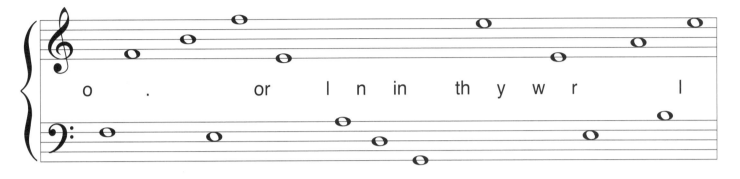

o   .   or l   n   in   th y w r   l

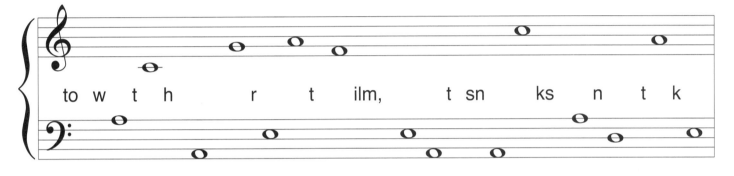

to w   t   h   r   t   ilm,   t sn   ks   n   t   k

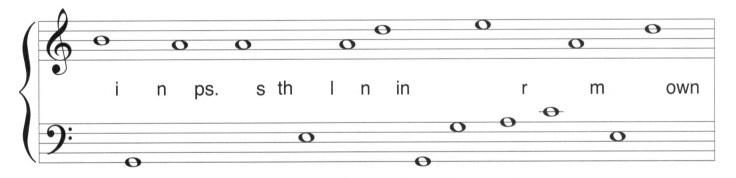

i   n   ps.   s th   l   n   in   r   m   own

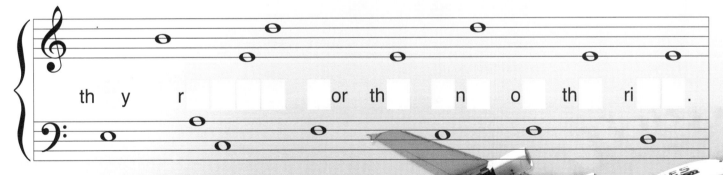

th y   r   or th   n   o   th   ri   .

TREBLE AND BASS LINE AND SPACE NOTES
Where in the World Is Half Note Harry?

1. Name the notes to complete the story.

2. Draw a stem for each note to make it a half note. The stems should go in the proper direction.

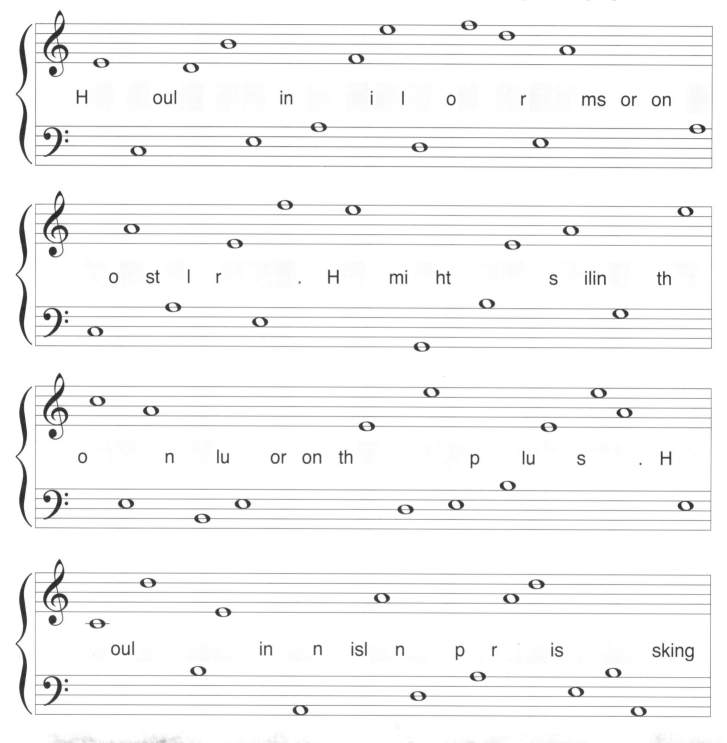

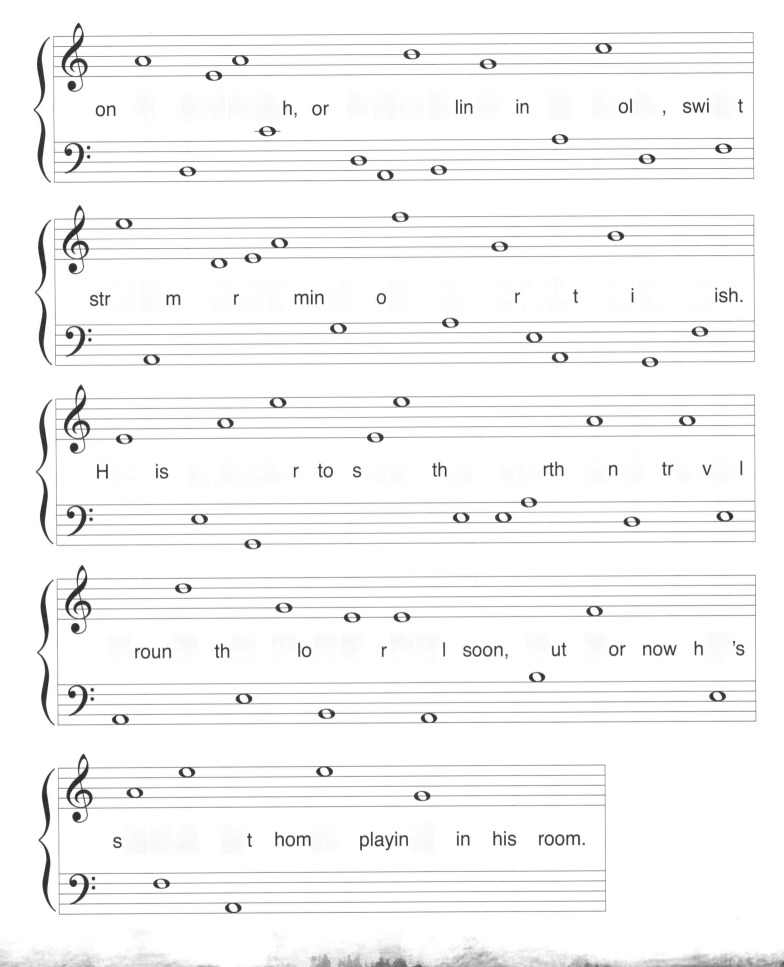

INTERVALS—4THS AND 5THS
George and Fred Go Hiking

1. Name the notes in this story.

2. Circle the 4ths and 5ths.

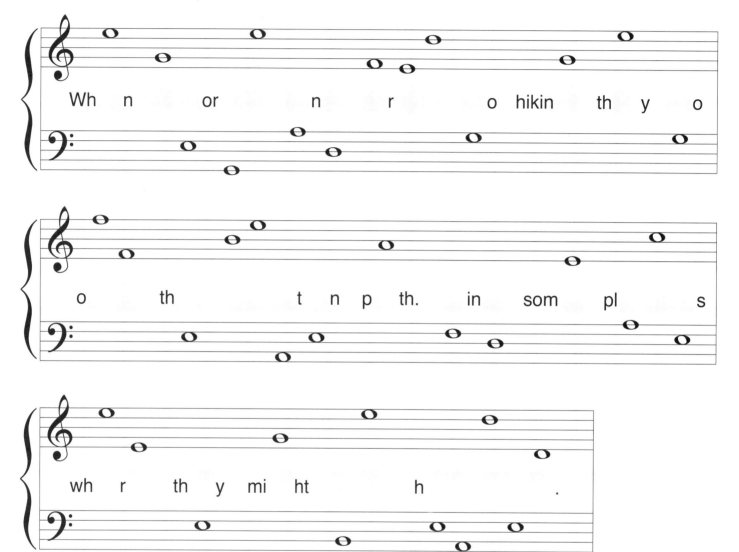

Below are places where George and Fred might choose to visit or attend.

1. Name the notes to spell the words.

2. Write 4th or 5th below every "?" that connects two notes.

s   ll   m   ik   p   th

?   ?   ?   ?

___   ___   ___   ___

r i   i   S   l   t   S

?   ?   ?

___   ___   ___

n   i   n   l   i   r

?   ?

___   ___

r   v   l   Ro   r   k   Isl   n

?   ?   ?

___   ___   ___

INTERVALS—2NDS THROUGH 6THS
Sports Around the World

Many of the world's sports are listed in the measures below.

1. Solve the crossword clues by naming the notes.
2. Name the intervals under every "?" that connects two notes.
3. Complete the crossword puzzle.

TREBLE AND BASS LINE AND SPACE NOTES
World Cuisine

Write the names of the notes in the shaded boxes to discover foods eaten by people from around the world.

Africa

r n M li r o oti T in

(corn pudding)   (lamb casserole)   (stew)

Australia and New Zealand

rp t r St k mp r r

Belgium and the Netherlands

Stu n iv u r tin u r s

(waffles)

Spain and Portugal

l o ll o m s on S ls V r

(sausage and vegetable soup)   (shrimp with green sauce)

Eastern Europe

Hun ri n Stu u l nin

(cherry cake)

Africa

Or n ___ hi k n ___ n ro oli ri Ri

France

rio h ___ hi k n ___ ri ss ___ Sou l ___ l m ___ s

Latin America

St ___ k R n h ros ___ n hil ___ s u ___ mol T ___ os

Italy

___ Si ili n ___ Ri ott ___ no ___ i ___ olo n s ___

India

S ___ P n ___ r S kh K ___ o ___ R it N ___ n ___ l

(spinach and cheese)   (lamb on a stick)   (yogurt sauce)   (bread)   (lentils)

31

TREBLE AND BASS LINE AND SPACE NOTES
A Poem for World Peace

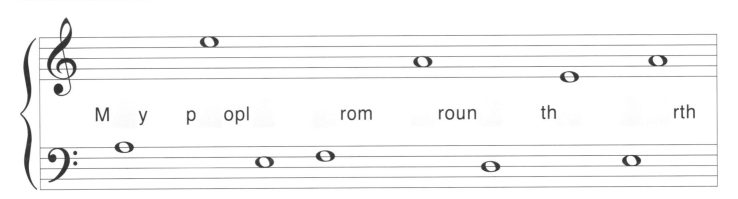

M y p opl   rom   roun   th   rth

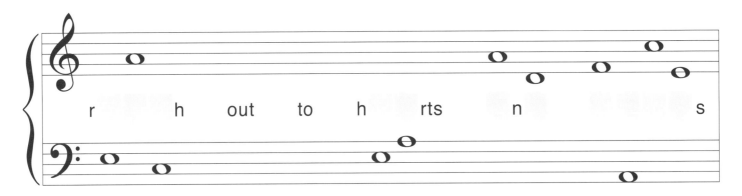

r   h   out   to   h rts   n   s

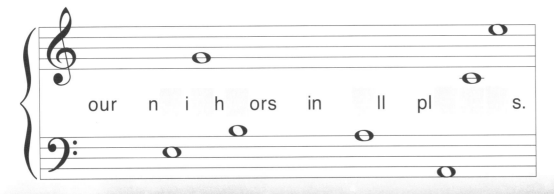

to   rin   worl   o   p   to   ll

our   n i h ors   in   ll pl   s.